NATIONAL GEOGRAPHIC

I Like Being Outdoors

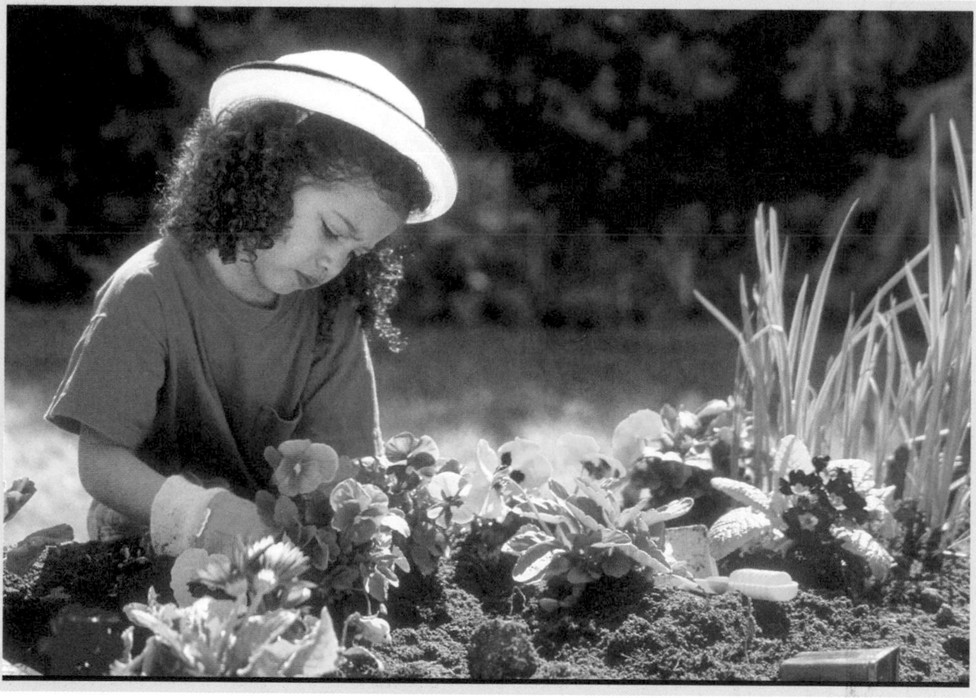

Wil Spencer

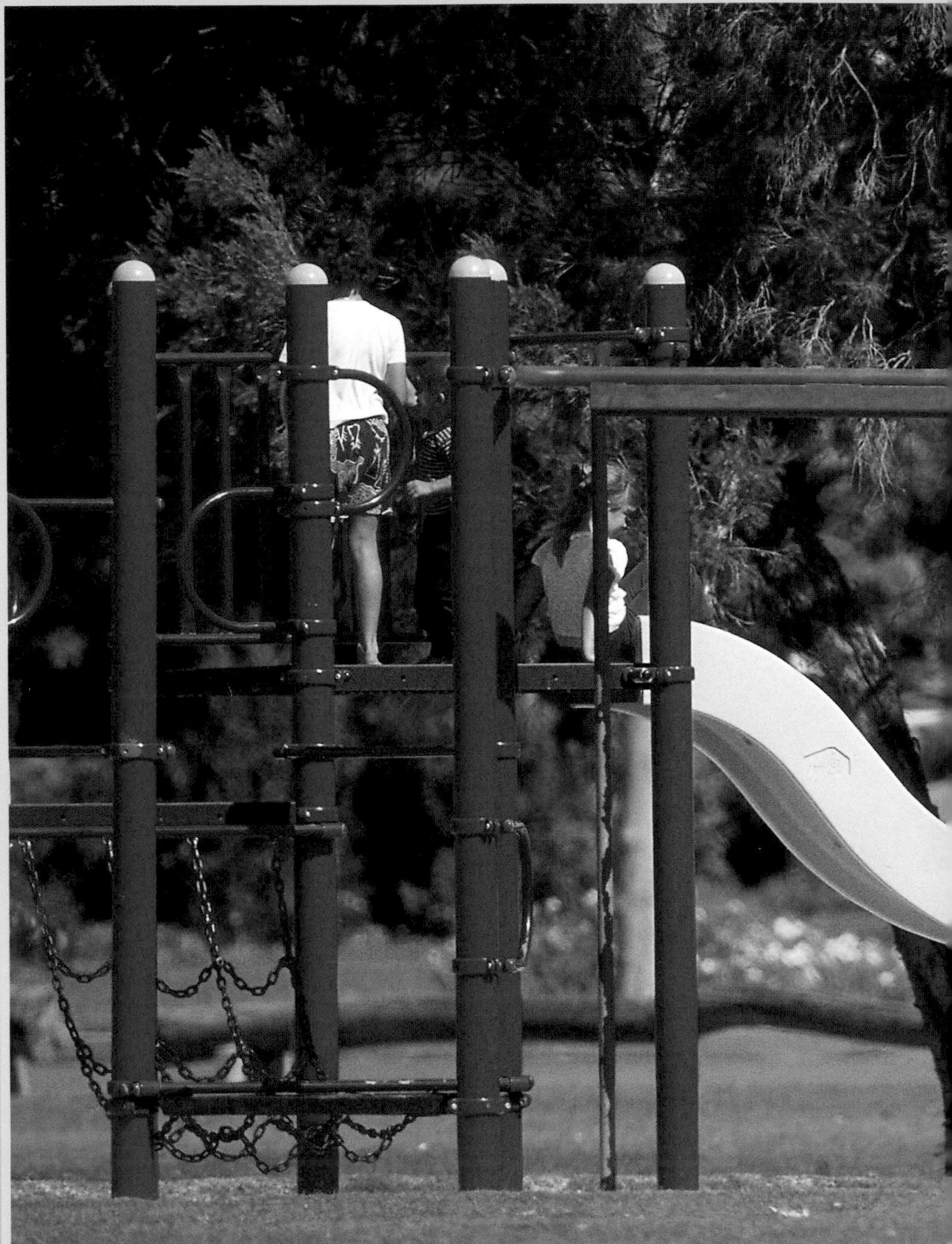

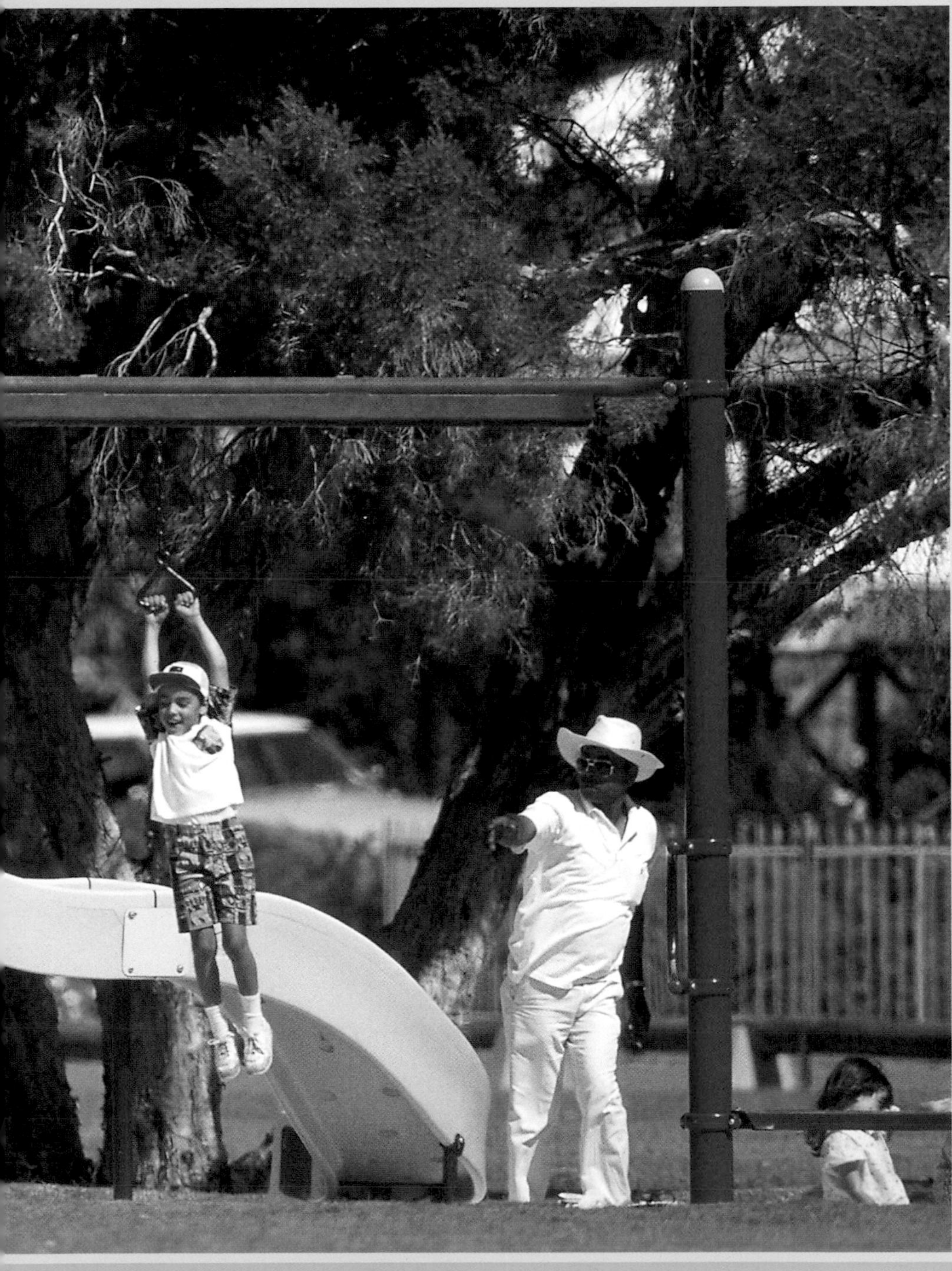

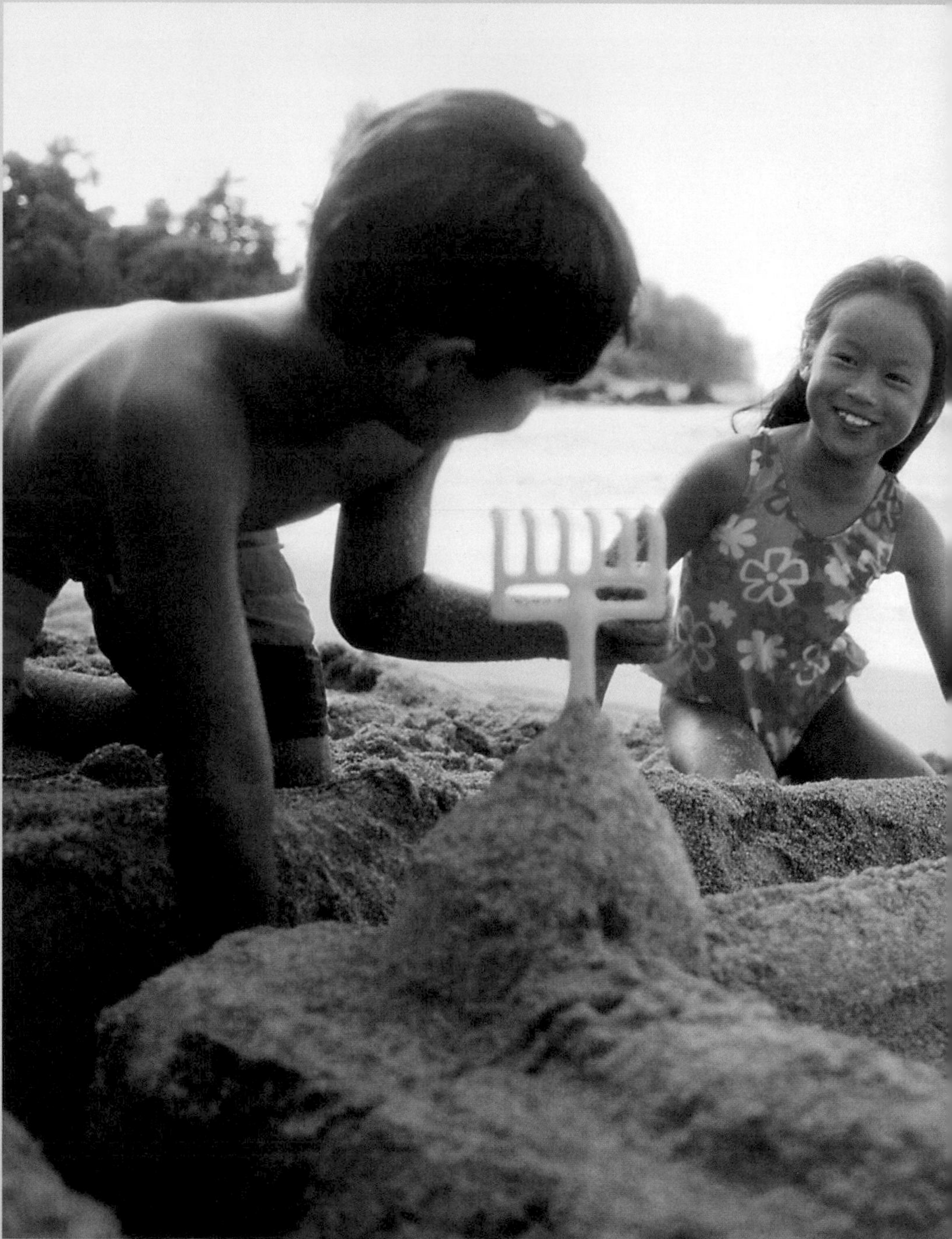

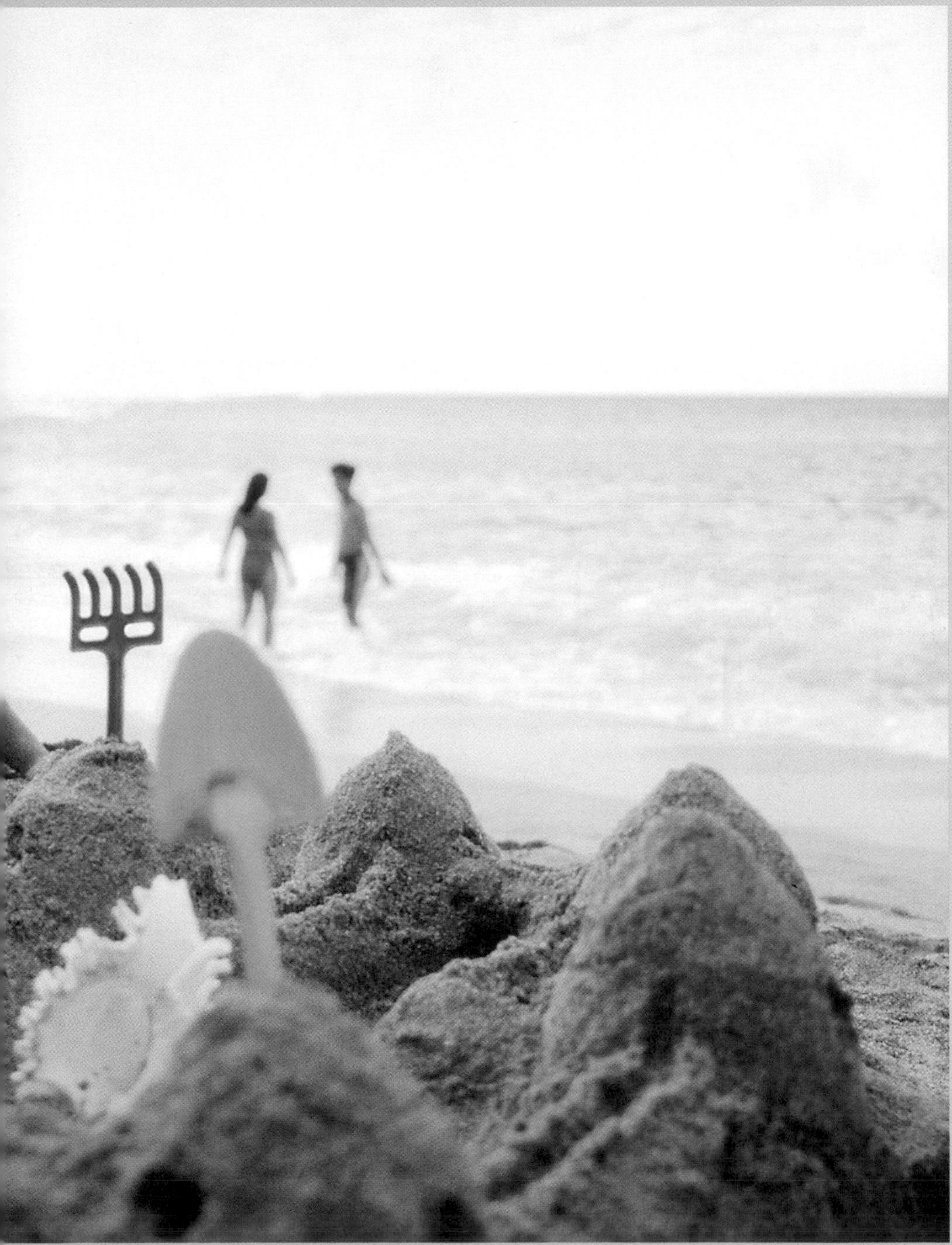

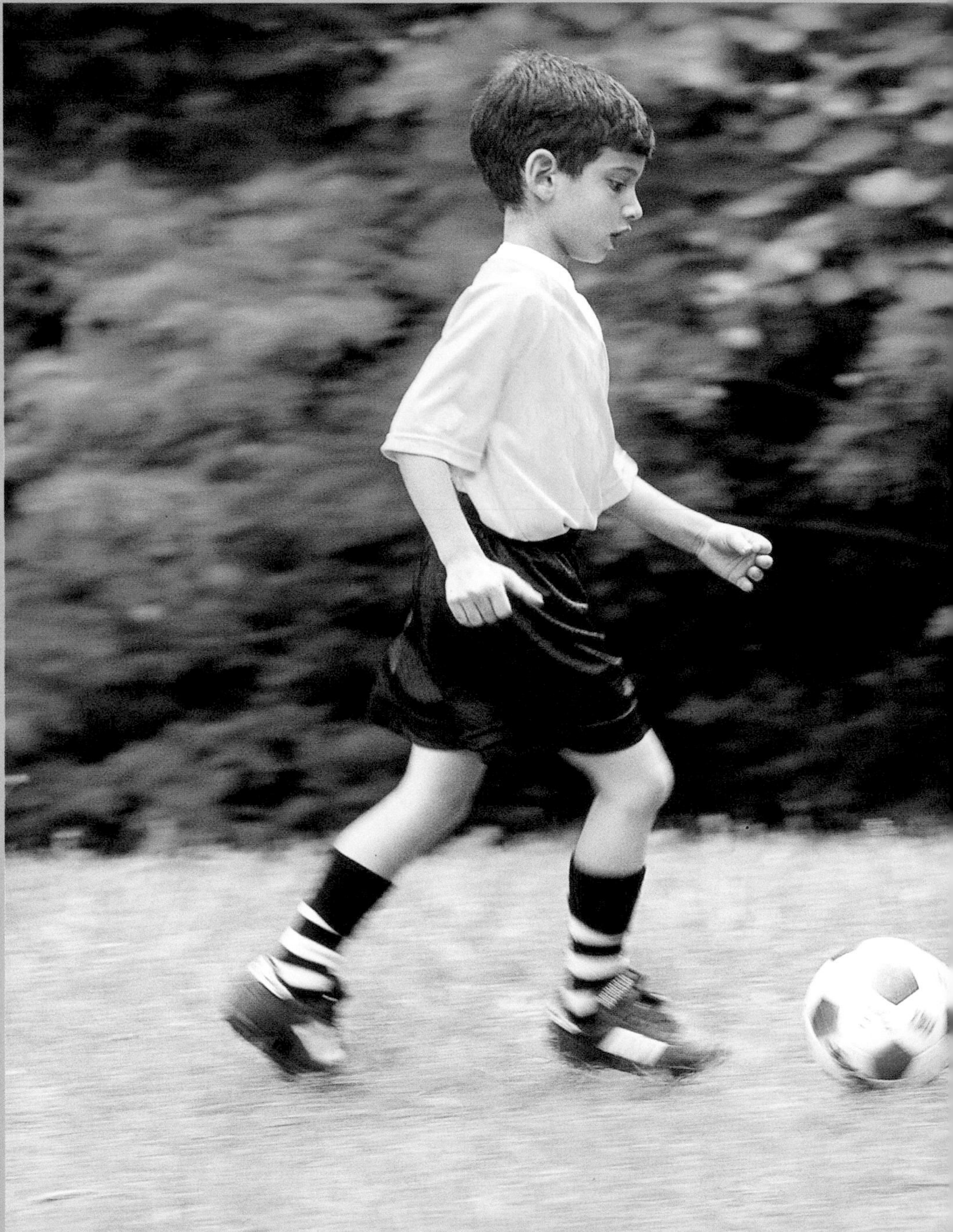

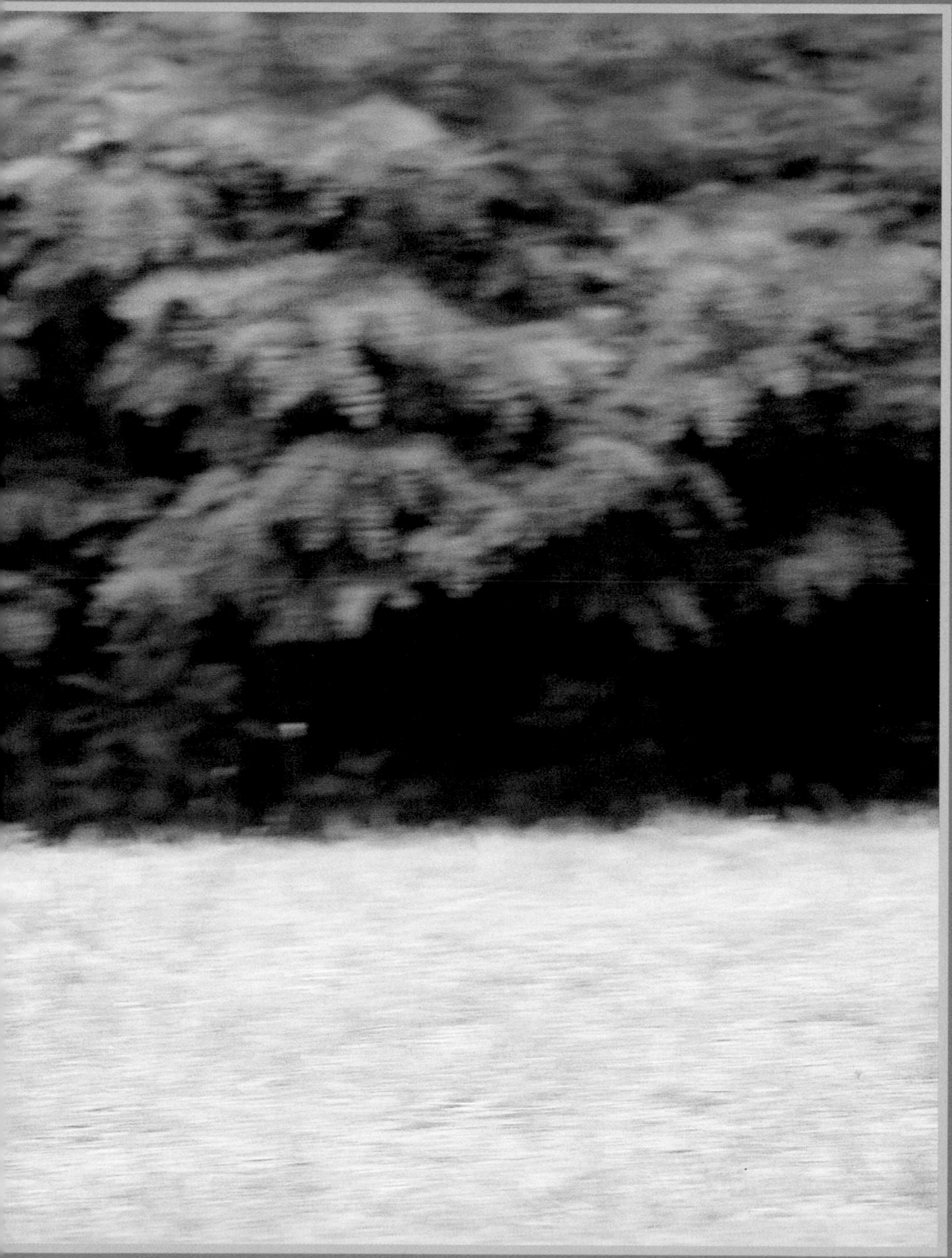

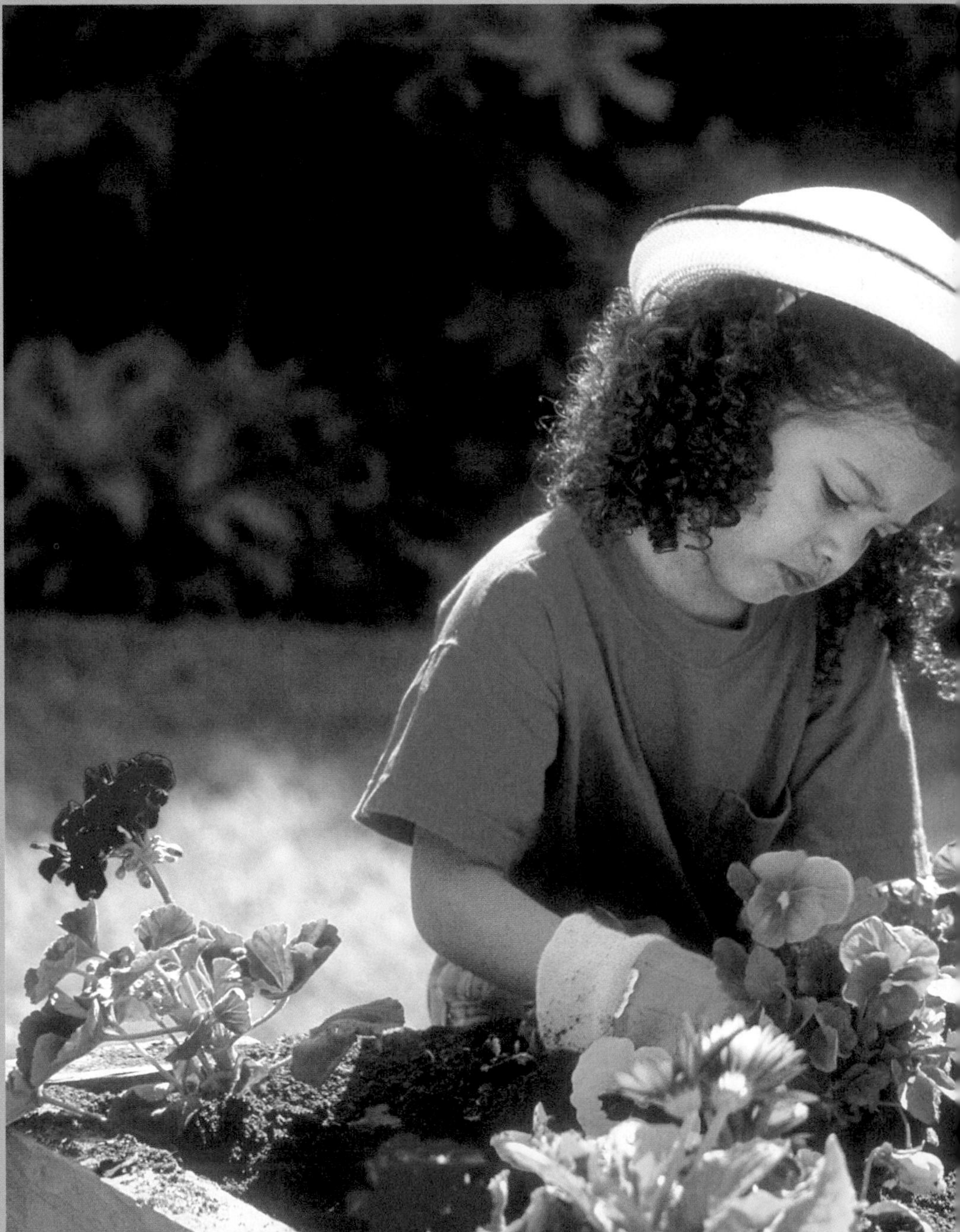

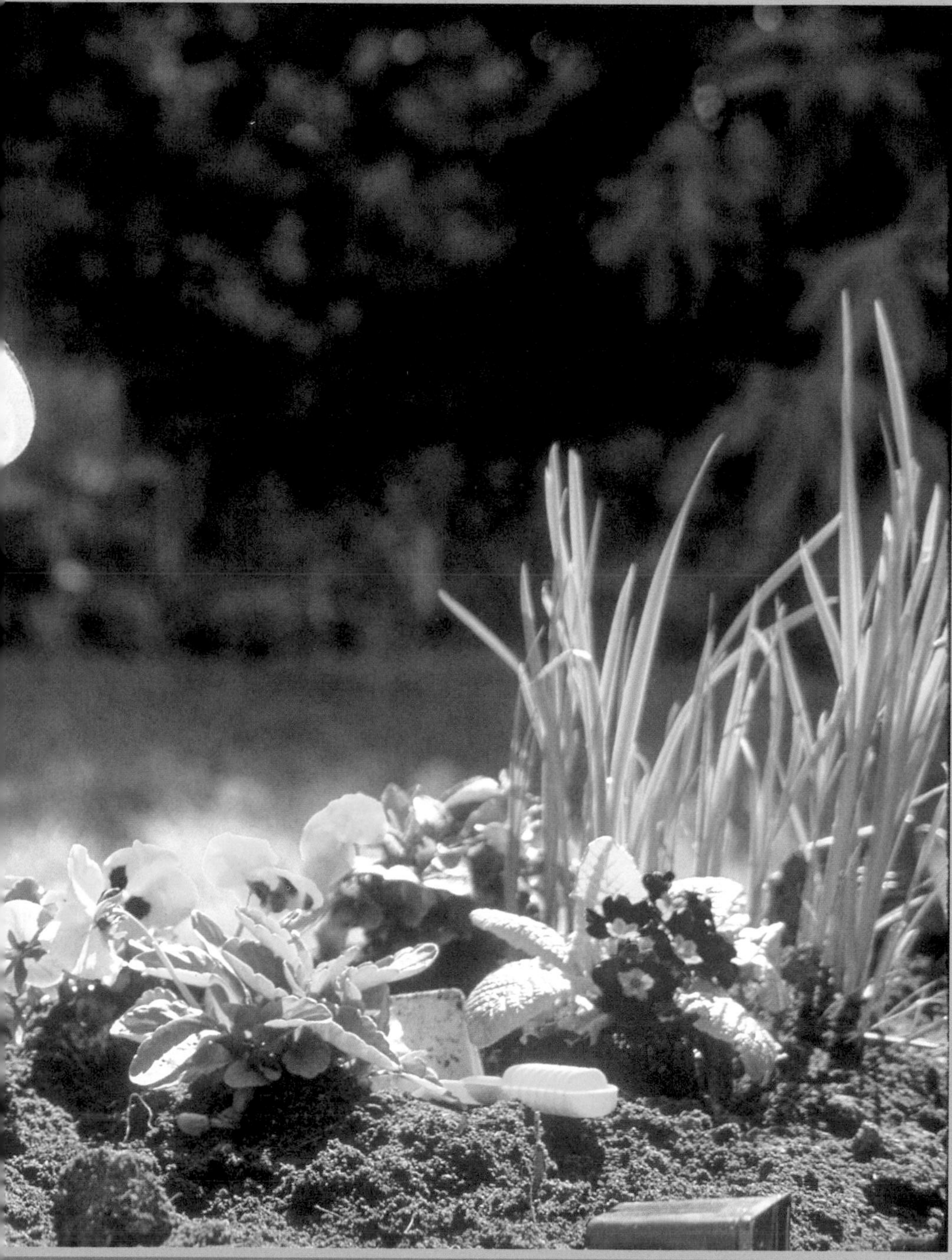

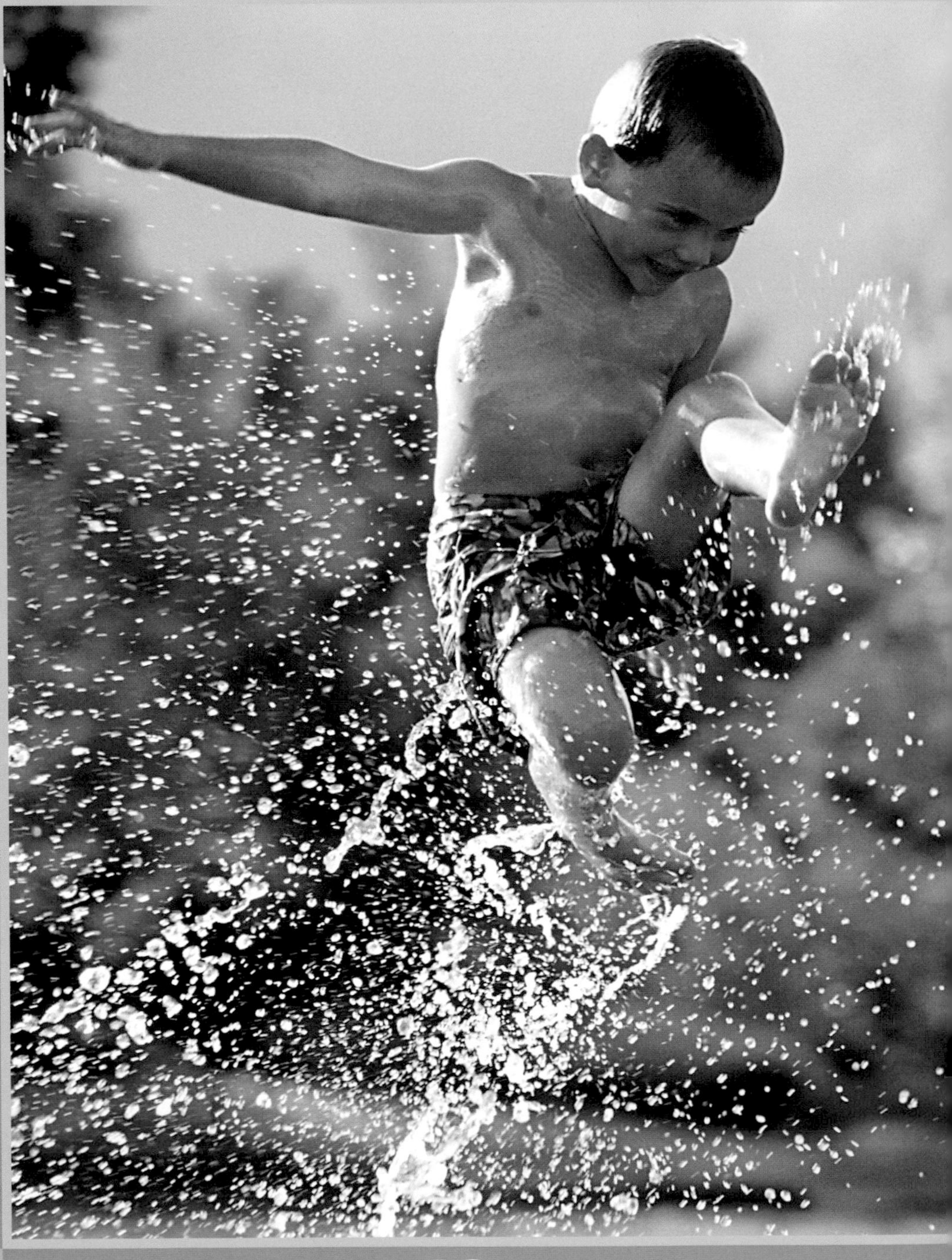

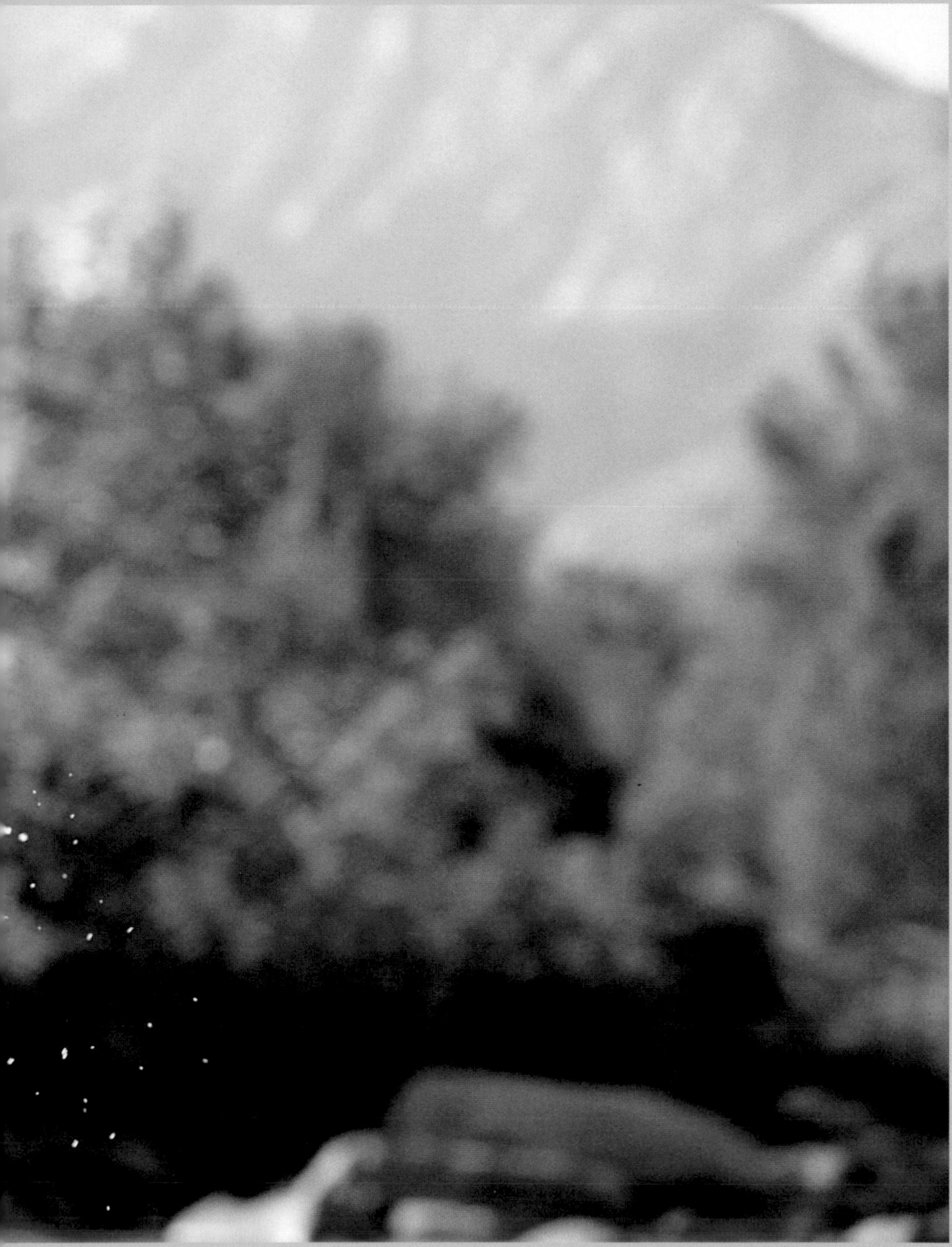

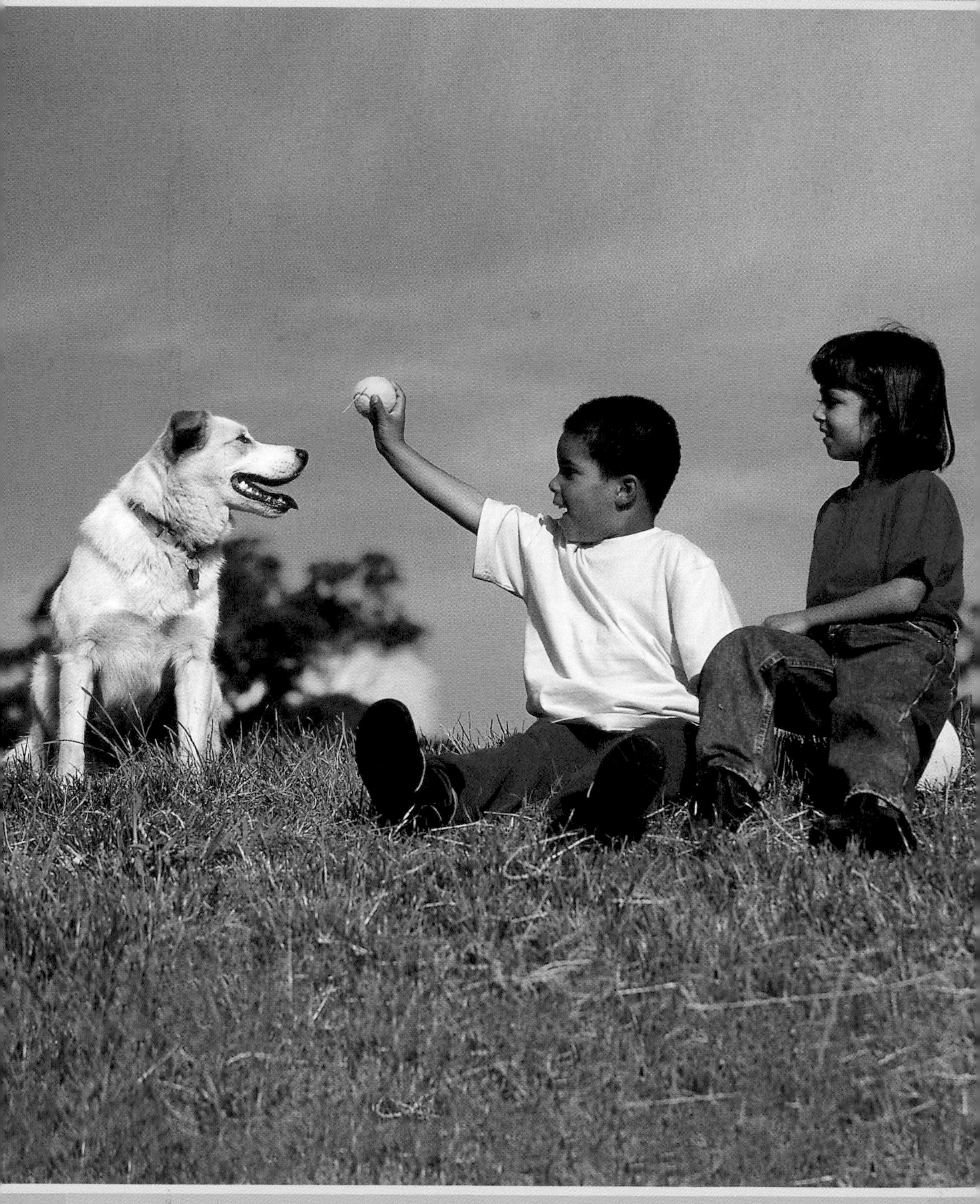